ALTO SAX

HAL•LEONARD
INSTRUMENTAL
PLAY-ALONG

AUDIO
ACCESS
INCLUDED

PLAYBACK+
Pitch • Balance • Loop

JAZZ BLUES FAVORITES

Audio arrangements by Peter Deneff

To access audio visit:
www.halleonard.com/mylibrary

Enter Code
5254-5531-0264-2861

ISBN 978-1-4950-5337-5

7777 W. BLUEMOUND RD. P.O. BOX 13819 MILWAUKEE, WI 53213

For all works contained herein:
Unauthorized copying, arranging, adapting, recording, Internet posting, public performance,
or other distribution of the printed or recorded music in this publication is an infringement of copyright.
Infringers are liable under the law.

Visit Hal Leonard Online at
www.halleonard.com

ALL BLUES

ALTO SAX

By MILES DAV¹

Copyright © 1959 Jazz Horn Music Corporation and Miles Davis Properties LLC
Copyright Renewed
All Rights Administered by Songs Of Kobalt Music Publishing
All Rights Reserved   Used by Permission

D.S. al Coda
(no repeat)

CODA

BASIN STREET BLUES

ALTO SAX

Words and Music by
SPENCER WILLIAMS

© 1928, 1929, 1933 (Renewed) EDWIN H. MORRIS & COMPANY, A Division of MPL Music Publishing, Inc.
All Rights Reserved

BIRK'S WORKS

LTO SAX

By DIZZY GILLESPIE

© 1957 (Renewed 1985) DIZLO MUSIC
All Rights Controlled and Administered by EMI APRIL MUSIC INC.
All Rights Reserved   International Copyright Secured   Used by Permission

C-JAM BLUES

ALTO SAX

By DUKE ELLINGTON

Copyright © 1942 Sony/ATV Music Publishing LLC in the U.S.A.
Copyright Renewed
All Rights Administered by Sony/ATV Music Publishing LLC, 424 Church Street, Suite 1200, Nashville, TN 37219
Rights for the world outside the U.S.A. Administered by EMI Robbins Catalog Inc. (Publishing) and Alfred Music (Print)
International Copyright Secured   All Rights Reserved

FREDDIE FREELOADER

ALTO SAX

By MILES DAVIS

Copyright © 1959 Jazz Horn Music Corporation
Copyright Renewed
All Rights Worldwide Administered by Songs Of Kobalt Music Publishing
All Rights Reserved   Used by Permission

MR. P.C.

ALTO SAX

By JOHN COLTRANE

Copyright © 1977 (Renewed) JOWCOL MUSIC LLC
International Copyright Secured   All Rights Reserved

NIGHT TRAIN

ALTO SAX

Words by OSCAR WASHINGTON
and LEWIS C. SIMPKINS
Music by JIMMY FORREST

Copyright © 1952 (Renewed) by Embassy Music Corporation (BMI)
International Copyright Secured   All Rights Reserved
Reprinted by Permission

NOW'S THE TIME

ALTO SAX

By CHARLIE PARKER

Copyright © 1945 (Renewed 1973) Atlantic Music Corp.
All Rights for the World excluding the U.S. Controlled and Administered by Screen Gems-EMI Music Inc.
International Copyright Secured   All Rights Reserved

ONE FOR DADDY-O

ALTO SAX

By NAT ADDERLY

© 1958 (Renewed) by DILLARD MUSIC
All Rights Reserved   Used by Permission

THE SWINGIN' SHEPHERD BLUES

ALTO SAX

Words and Music by MOE KOFFMAN,
RHODA ROBERTS and KENNY JACOBSON

© 1958 (Renewed 1986) EMI LONGITUDE MUSIC
All Rights Reserved   International Copyright Secured   Used by Permission

TENOR MADNESS

ALTO SAX

By SONNY ROLLINS

Copyright © 1956, 1980 Prestige Music
Copyright Renewed
International Copyright Secured   All Rights Reserved

THINGS AIN'T WHAT THEY USED TO BE

ALTO SAX

By MERCER ELLINGTON

Copyright © 1942, 1964 (Renewed) by Tempo Music, Inc. and Music Sales Corporation (ASCAP)
All Rights Administered by Music Sales Corporation
International Copyright Secured   All Rights Reserved
Reprinted by Permission

HAL•LEONARD INSTRUMENTAL PLAY-ALONG

Your favorite songs are arranged just for solo instrumentalists with this outstanding series. Each book includes a great full-accompaniment play-along audio so you can sound just like a pro! Check out www.halleonard.com to see all the titles available.

Chart Hits

All About That Bass • All of Me • Happy • Radioactive • Roar • Say Something • Shake It Off • A Sky Full of Stars • Someone like You • Stay with Me • Thinking Out Loud • Uptown Funk.

_____00146207 Flute $12.99
_____00146208 Clarinet $12.99
_____00146209 Alto Sax $12.99
_____00146210 Tenor Sax $12.99
_____00146211 Trumpet. $12.99
_____00146212 Horn $12.99
_____00146213 Trombone $12.99
_____00146214 Violin. $12.99
_____00146215 Viola $12.99
_____00146216 Cello $12.99

Coldplay

Clocks • Every Teardrop Is a Waterfall • Fix You • In My Place • Lost! • Paradise • The Scientist • Speed of Sound • Trouble • Violet Hill • Viva La Vida • Yellow.

_____00103337 Flute $12.99
_____00103338 Clarinet $12.99
_____00103339 Alto Sax $12.99
_____00103340 Tenor Sax $12.99
_____00103341 Trumpet. $12.99
_____00103342 Horn $12.99
_____00103343 Trombone $12.99
_____00103344 Violin. $12.99
_____00103345 Viola $12.99
_____00103346 Cello $12.99

Disney Greats

Arabian Nights • Hawaiian Roller Coaster Ride • It's a Small World • Look Through My Eyes • Yo Ho (A Pirate's Life for Me) • and more.

_____00841934 Flute $12.99
_____00841935 Clarinet $12.99
_____00841936 Alto Sax $12.99
_____00841937 Tenor Sax $12.95
_____00841938 Trumpet. $12.99
_____00841939 Horn $12.95
_____00841940 Trombone $12.95
_____00841941 Violin. $12.99
_____00841942 Viola $12.95
_____00841943 Cello $12.99
_____00842078 Oboe. $12.99

Great Themes

Bella's Lullaby • Chariots of Fire • Get Smart • Hawaii Five-O Theme • I Love Lucy • The Odd Couple • Spanish Flea • and more.

_____00842468 Flute $12.99
_____00842469 Clarinet $12.99
_____00842470 Alto Sax $12.99
_____00842471 Tenor Sax $12.99
_____00842472 Trumpet. $12.99
_____00842473 Horn $12.99
_____00842474 Trombone $12.99
_____00842475 Violin. $12.99
_____00842476 Viola $12.99
_____00842477 Cello $12.99

Lennon & McCartney Favorites

All You Need Is Love • A Hard Day's Night • Here, There and Everywhere • Hey Jude • Let It Be • Nowhere Man • Penny Lane • She Loves You • When I'm Sixty-Four • and more.

_____00842600 Flute $12.99
_____00842601 Clarinet $12.99
_____00842603 Tenor Sax $12.99
_____00842604 Trumpet. $12.99
_____00842605 Horn $12.99
_____00842607 Violin. $12.99
_____00842608 Viola $12.99
_____00842609 Cello $12.99

Popular Hits

Breakeven • Fireflies • Halo • Hey, Soul Sister • I Gotta Feeling • I'm Yours • Need You Now • Poker Face • Viva La Vida • You Belong with Me • and more.

_____00842511 Flute $12.99
_____00842512 Clarinet $12.99
_____00842513 Alto Sax $12.99
_____00842514 Tenor Sax $12.99
_____00842515 Trumpet. $12.99
_____00842516 Horn $12.99
_____00842517 Trombone $12.99
_____00842518 Violin. $12.99
_____00842519 Viola $12.99
_____00842520 Cello $12.99

Songs from Frozen, Tangled and Enchanted

Do You Want to Build a Snowman? • For the First Time in Forever • Happy Working Song • I See the Light • In Summer • Let It Go • Mother Knows Best • That's How You Know • True Love's First Kiss • When Will My Life Begin • and more.

_____00126921 Flute $14.99
_____00126922 Clarinet $14.99
_____00126923 Alto Sax $14.99
_____00126924 Tenor Sax $14.99
_____00126925 Trumpet. $14.99
_____00126926 Horn $14.99
_____00126927 Trombone $14.99
_____00126928 Violin. $14.99
_____00126929 Viola $14.99
_____00126930 Cello $14.99

Top Hits

Adventure of a Lifetime • Budapest • Die a Happy Man • Ex's & Oh's • Fight Song • Hello • Let It Go • Love Yourself • One Call Away • Pillowtalk • Stitches • Writing's on the Wall.

_____00171073 Flute $12.99
_____00171074 Clarinet $12.99
_____00171075 Alto Sax $12.99
_____00171106 Tenor Sax $12.99
_____00171107 Trumpet. $12.99
_____00171108 Horn $12.99
_____00171109 Trombone $12.99
_____00171110 Violin. $12.99
_____00171111 Viola $12.99
_____00171112 Cello $12.99

Wicked

As Long As You're Mine • Dancing Through Life • Defying Gravity • For Good • I'm Not That Girl • Popular • The Wizard and I • and more.

_____00842236 Flute $12.99
_____00842237 Clarinet $11.99
_____00842238 Alto Saxophone $11.95
_____00842239 Tenor Saxophone. $11.95
_____00842240 Trumpet. $11.99
_____00842241 Horn $11.95
_____00842242 Trombone $12.99
_____00842243 Violin. $11.99
_____00842244 Viola $12.99
_____00842245 Cello $12.99

Prices, contents, and availability subject to change without notice.
Disney characters and artwork © Disney Enterprises, Inc.

HAL•LEONARD®

101 SONGS

YOUR FAVORITE SONGS ARE ARRANGED FOR SOLO INSTRUMENTALISTS WITH THIS GREAT SERIES.

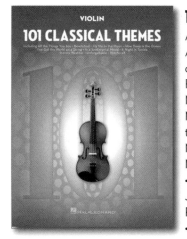

FLUTE
101 BROADWAY SONGS

101 BROADWAY SONGS

Cabaret • Do You Hear the People Sing? • Edelweiss • Guys and Dolls • Hello, Dolly! • I Dreamed a Dream • If I Were a Bell • Luck Be a Lady • Ol' Man River • Seasons of Love • Send in the Clowns • Think of Me • Tomorrow • What I Did for Love • and many more.

00154199	Flute	$14.99
00154200	Clarinet	$14.99
00154201	Alto Sax	$14.99
00154202	Tenor Sax	$14.99
00154203	Trumpet	$14.99
00154204	Horn	$14.99
00154205	Trombone	$14.99
00154206	Violin	$14.99
00154207	Viola	$14.99
00154208	Cello	$14.99

CELLO
101 HIT SONGS

101 HIT SONGS

All About That Bass • All of Me • Brave • Breakaway • Clocks • Fields of Gold • Firework • Hey, Soul Sister • Ho Hey • I Gotta Feeling • Jar of Hearts • Love Story • 100 Years • Roar • Rolling in the Deep • Shake It Off • Smells like Teen Spirit • Uptown Funk • and more.

00194561	Flute	$16.99
00197182	Clarinet	$16.99
00197183	Alto Sax	$16.99
00197184	Tenor Sax	$16.99
00197185	Trumpet	$16.99
00197186	Horn	$16.99
00197187	Trombone	$16.99
00197188	Violin	$16.99
00197189	Viola	$16.99
00197190	Cello	$16.99

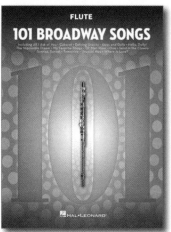

VIOLIN
101 CLASSICAL THEMES

101 CLASSICAL THEMES

Ave Maria • Bist du bei mir (You Are with Me) • Canon in D • Clair de Lune • Dance of the Sugar Plum Fairy • 1812 Overture • Eine Kleine Nachtmusik ("Serenade"), First Movement Excerpt • The Flight of the Bumble Bee • Funeral March of a Marionette • Fur Elise • Gymnopedie No. 1 • Jesu, Joy of Man's Desiring • Lullaby • Minuet in G • Ode to Joy • Piano Sonata in C • Pie Jesu • Rondeau • Theme from Swan Lake • Wedding March • William Tell Overture • and many more.

00155315	Flute	$14.99
00155317	Clarinet	$14.99
00155318	Alto Sax	$14.99
00155319	Tenor Sax	$14.99
00155320	Trumpet	$14.99
00155321	Horn	$14.99
00155322	Trombone	$14.99
00155323	Violin	$14.99
00155324	Viola	$14.99
00155325	Cello	$14.99

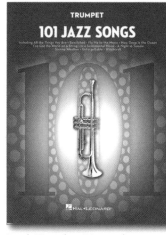

TRUMPET
101 JAZZ SONGS

101 JAZZ SONGS

All of Me • Autumn Leaves • Bewitched • Blue Skies • Body and Soul • Cheek to Cheek • Come Rain or Come Shine • Don't Get Around Much Anymore • A Fine Romance • Here's to Life • I Could Write a Book • It Could Happen to You • The Lady Is a Tramp • Like Someone in Love • Lullaby of Birdland • The Nearness of You • On Green Dolphin Street • Satin Doll • Stella by Starlight • Tangerine • Unforgettable • The Way You Look Tonight • Yesterdays • and many more.

00146363	Flute	$14.99
00146364	Clarinet	$14.99
00146366	Alto Sax	$14.99
00146367	Tenor Sax	$14.99
00146368	Trumpet	$14.99
00146369	Horn	$14.99
00146370	Trombone	$14.99
00146371	Violin	$14.99
00146372	Viola	$14.99
00146373	Cello	$14.99

HAL•LEONARD®

www.halleonard.com

Prices, contents and availability subject to change without notice.

O217